Planning To File For Divorce In Texas?

Know Your Options Before You Make The Decision That Impacts The Rest Of Your Life

Bobby Dale Barina, Esq.

ISBN: 978-1-941645-86-4

Designed and Published by:

Speakeasy Publications

73-03 Bell Blvd #10

Oakland Gardens, NY 11364

888-225-8594

www.SpeakeasyMarketingInc.com

DISCLAIMER

This publication is intended to be informational only. The information in this book is not intended as legal advice. No legal advice is being given, and no attorney-client relationship is intended to be created by reading this material. If you are facing legal issues, whether criminal or civil, seek professional legal counsel to get your questions answered.

Bobby Dale Barina,

455 E. Central Texas Expy

Suite 104

Harker Heights, TX 76548

(254) 870-9947

www.yourkilleendivorceattorney.com

TESTIMONIALS

"I used Mr. Barina as my attorney in a child custody case earlier this year. He did a good job of letting me know what needed to be done to get the child support adjusted for my son. His staff was extremely helpful when Mr. Barina was otherwise indisposed, and they knew what was going on every time I asked. I appreciate the team effort put forward by Mr. Barina and his employees. His associate attorney even went to court one time when I couldn't and that saved having to get the case reset which would have taken longer. I appreciate everything you all did for me. Thank you."

- Laura

"Mr. Barina is a top-rated attorney in Bell County, Texas. His practice extends to family law, juvenile crime defense, and adult crime defense. He is very knowledgeable about the law and how to use the law strategically to achieve the best possible result for his client. He is one of a very few lawyers in the Bell County area to have ever been ranked as a Texas Super Lawyer in any category by Texas Monthly Magazine."

- Michelle O.

"Finally it's over and we won the case. Really want to thank the BDB Attorney for their continuous support. I never thought that we can win the case in this short time, their documentation and presentation of the proof and other support files in the court was really amazing."

- Ida E.

"Mr. Barina and the staff were very helpful all through the divorce and custody. They handled my case and I was very pleased with the outcome. The key to quality and efficiency is professionalism, and that is what Mr. Barina delivered."

- A Former Client

"Bobby helped me greatly! He help me through the most stressful time of my life!"

- Marla

TABLE OF CONTENTS

Author Introduction

I'm board certified in both family law and criminal law, and I've tried cases in every area of my practice. While there are many Texas lawyers who can boast of experience, what sets my firm apart is personal service. Personally handling every case that comes into my office, I'll prepare your case from the opening.

My areas of practice include

- ✓ Family Law
- ✓ Criminal Law
- ✓ Custody & Visitation
- ✓ DUI/DWI
- ✓ Divorce
- ✓ Adoption
- ✓ Child Support

Divorce – An Overview

The decisions you make in your divorce will impact the rest of your life. Many people decide to approach divorce as a fight, but an experienced lawyer can help you take a deep breath, stay focused on your long-term goals and reach solutions without a costly and time-consuming fight.

When people are in a bad emotional state, they often make bad financial decisions. It is an attorney's job to help you avoid decisions that could be disastrous down the road. Helping you explore your full range of settlement options, including divorce mediation, your attorney will help you find solutions without a fight. However, he will also be ready to protect your rights in court, if necessary.

Taking a look at the wide range of factors that will impact your case, your attorney will help you understand what to expect from every aspect of your divorce, including:

Child Custody and Support: Children must be treated with kindness and understanding during the divorce process. Talking to your children face to face, your attorney will help them get their minds in the right place, so you can work as a family on a custody plan that works.

Property Division: Always aiming for the fair and equitable division of assets, your attorney will protect your financial future and help you explore your full range of options.

Spousal Support: There is a three-year life span for spousal support in Texas, but your attorney can help you come up with a plan that makes sense during that time.

ISSUES THAT NEED TO BE DEALT WITH IN A DIVORCE CASE

Custody is the biggest issue, and retirement is right behind it, but that deals with the parties. In custody matters, several things have to be considered, for example how that thing is arranged or how it's for the child's best interest as well as the parents, and you need an attorney on that.

When you look at the Texas family code on our standard provisions, you go from 35 percent up to 41 percent based on the options you pick. Most people don't know their options because nobody explains that to them. And reading it to yourself, it is hard to figure out, and that's why you need an attorney to explain those options over how the children would get back and forth. So, you should never go without an attorney.

Do Clients Need To Have Some Closure From An Emotional Standpoint?

Yes. The closure happens over many months to years, and you don't want to really go back to it.

There is an old story that can be shared here. When they were looking at pilots over the North Atlantic, the pilots could stay with the plane if it was going down, and they would die. But they're in a small confined area that they're used to. If the pilots bailed out with the existing resources and the wet suits they had and the pressure suits and the rest, they could survive in that freezing water up to 15 minutes. And variably, they all chose to stay in the cockpit because it's what they knew. People are afraid of the unknown because there is so much uncertainty, and that's really the biggest reason to hire a lawyer.

For most clients, this is their first, possibly their second divorce. But for an attorney, it is literally the thousandth. Attorneys have been there before. They have seen people in all kinds of situations. While every case is unique, lawyers have an incredible amount of resources to draw upon to put a roadmap in front of the client on how this is going to proceed step by step. This is what attorneys are here for, to be your guide from the beginning to the end through what is the emotional process. An attorney can take the fear of the unknown of the divorce process out of the equation.

What Should A Person Do In Preparation For Divorce Or Separation?

You look at it in two different ways when you're entering the divorce process:

- Are you the one who made the decision?
- Are you the one who was confronted with the other person's decision?

If you're the one making the decision, you have to:

Figure out how you're going to survive, financially, but also start collecting things. You want to have access to all the financial records you can, because you need to have them immediately, and the debts. Debts and assets usually go together in financial.

You want as many photos as possible because once the emotional context gets into play, you don't want to have to be trying to ask an upset soon-to-be-ex spouse for photos of the children, for access to records, because that may be at home that you don't go back to.

You want to start figuring out the teachers who's involved. Most parents are already aware of that, but how the children are going to get back and forth to see each parent if they're not in the same home, if there's shift work involved.

The commingling debt, somebody has to be responsible for that debt, so that needs to be charted out but there are many processes to do but it's really one where you want to know how much resources you have and all the financial information possible.

If there are things regarding health, nowadays you can go online with different software from medical providers to pull the children's medical records. You want to make sure you have access to that, and so you have access to the doctors, to their medical history, things of that nature, but you need to plan it out very carefully.

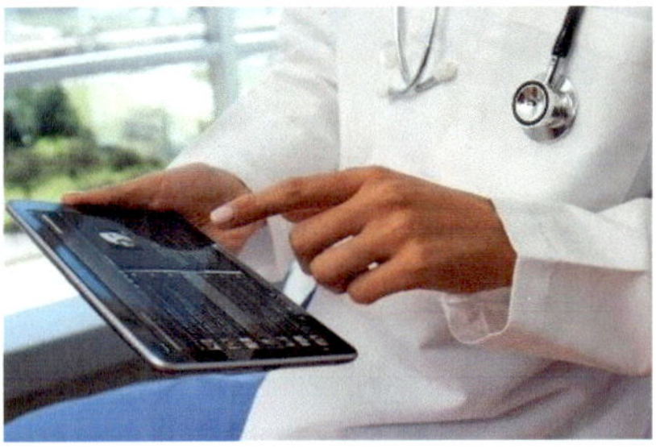

And there are many ways of doing it. The law office of Bobby Barina gives people the information that they need to start collecting for the divorce. If the client is responding, they are immediately asked go to the bank and start trying to access as many records as they can, go to the mortgage company if it's local, and sometimes those loans get sold and sold. And if that's the case, then the lawyers have somebody go down to the county clerk's office and look for the deed records, for the property records.

How Often Is A Request For Modification In A Divorce Lawsuit Seen?

Unfortunately, it's really strange in the modification world. The first question to look at is what do you want to change, and then the attorneys start looking at the paperwork. It is surprising how often attorneys represent somebody in a modification that they did not represent on the underlying lawsuit, the underlying divorce, the underlying petition to establish the parent-child relationship and to establish child support that they want.

The first child support comes up every 3 to 4 years if the parties aren't staying in close contact. Then, you have to see if that party's entitled to more child support. But honestly, if they're going to be entitled to $100 a month more and it's going to cost them a couple of thousand to find that out, that's not good business. There are things in the law that allow them to find out a little bit differently and an attorney will try to steer in that direction.

However, in custody, when the children get older and they start expressing themselves a little bit differently and they have a greater relationship with one party because of interests; for instance, if one party lives on a farm and the child wants to be a farmer, the attorney can see where custody would have to be modified. Sometimes parents are able to make their decisions themselves, sometimes they're not, in which case attorneys will go to court and let the child express their thoughts to the judge privately. But that's really it.

Attorneys look at child support, they look at visitation that has to be tinkered with, they look at electronic communication, which is something older divorce decrees didn't have because they didn't have Skype, Hangout through Google, or FaceTime on their phones to allow people to communicate, but they like to add those in there.

In most cases, there's always some tweaking to be done on the peripheral as long as it's not leading into re-opening the old wounds and attorneys are just trying to make things better, advocate it a lot, but that's the reason; visitation. What if one party moves from being around the street, around the corner from one parent, and they move 2,000 miles away? Then the attorney will have to go back to court to modify how that child gets there.

For instance, there is the Long Distance Provision. Attorneys make sure that one parent who has the child or children goes to the airport to meet the other parent. And the reason for that is when that parent comes in from the other location, they don't have to rent a car, drive an hour to the house, pick up the children, drive back, go through baggage, and go through everything else. The children are already there, they simply walk out, walk back in with all the tickets, the required security, clearance and move on.

Long Distance Provision saves hours and hours of frustration and the children have a good understanding of what's going on or when the children are old enough to travel by themselves, somebody still has to take them to the airport. Visitation has to be modified a little bit off and on to allow for that, and electronic communication is not a replacement, but can be a supplement to visitation that is utilized.

To add to this, looking at the military deployments, what if a soldier, be it a male or female, suddenly has to rapidly deploy because of their job specialty? The office of Bobby Barina has deployed people who have special skill sets around the world. One group was deployed for the first time in decades because of what they do, but they had to deploy to a location in Africa because of the possible Ebola spread, so they deployed, and there had to be a provision for their family to see the children in their absence.

Their parents had to establish and keep that relationship going, that connection with that side of the family, because it's best for the children and it's best for the parent to know their children are still involved in their life. The office of Bobby Barina does that as well.

Divorce Laws And Common Law Marriage In Texas

The State of Texas recognizes the Common Law Marriage. There are 13 states that recognize it. Common law really comes from the point, way back in the horse and buggy days, when you didn't see a JP or a judge or somebody who had the authority to do a marriage because it took you months to get the nearest county.

They had these ways of saying to the world, "We are married." We've had common law in Texas ever since the 1800s when first we were dealing with not just common law marriage, and some people call it informal marriage, but we had the common law. We had things that just developed based on common needs, and so that was surely one of them. There were three steps to common law marriage:

- You have to be in Texas;
- You have to hold yourself out as husband and wife, and
- You have to do it at the same time.

The male and the female would say to others at the same time, “We are married. This is a union we wish to be involved in, and for all purposes we are married.”

Is There A Certain Time Period A Couple Has To Be Together To Establish Their Common Law Marriage?

Oddly enough, no. They can simply get together and say, “This is what we’re going to do.” You think about it in the plain days when the trains would stop at the local train depot and the mail-order brides would get off. They were looking at the union rank and they wanted to express themselves to the world, so there is no timeframe. It’s simply those three acts.

There are pieces of evidence that go with it if it becomes contested; how long they were living together is truly one of the most important details if somebody contests a common law marriage. But if they were to write it down, and you can file a declaration with the district clerk in whichever clerk’s office in any other counties that have jurisdiction over family law matters, you can do

that. You can simply show up together, notarize, file it, and you're good to go.

But here, as long as you hold it out and it's very clear what you're doing, you can do that on one day, two days or however long it takes for you to make that decision and that commitment.

How To Prove Two People Have Been In A Common Law Marriage When It Comes To Filing For Divorce?

When you break it down, one party is trying to say, "We are common law married," and the other party is trying to say, "We're not." So, we go through just the list of evidentiary concerns. How long were they together, how long did they live together, did they ever have a ceremony? Maybe not a ceremony presided by a judge or somebody who'd been ordained, but somebody that's been given authority by the state to perform services.

Did you have or have a service otherwise, a party, a celebration? Did you exchange things that were meaningful, be it a ring, or a gift of some kind? Remember, some people used to trade farm animals to accomplish this. So the question is, how did you present to the world that you were one unit legally?

Lawyers at Bobby Barina's firm go down through this long list of tests to try to show what the agreement was, who witnessed the agreement, and how was the agreement detailed to others. Then they look at cohabitation, the existence of a ceremony of some kind, and if they have an agreement, who was there.

When you hold yourself out as husband and wife, everybody does it differently. Some people hold hands, some people are affectionate in public, some people kiss, some people will say, "Yes, we are the children's parents," and so

an attorney will look at all of that and in Texas, a jury can decide that issue of if there was a common law and then if there was, here is the divorce.

It's an interesting process. There are factors to consider, such as whether things like salary contracts, the purchase of real estate, investments, and other things occurred during the common law marriage. So, attorneys really do have to take a good look at all that.

Does It Require Some Digging And Research?

Yes. Usually, lawyers render the taxes first to say how they filed the taxes, and then they look at loan documents, bank documents, how they had their checking accounts, the survivor benefit's insurance, and anything else that somebody requires you to include a spouse. And remember, for most health insurance, before the situation of same sex marriage, when you had insurance papers or you had family added to your health insurance, that was only for recognized marriages, not civil unions, so attorneys look at those really close too.

Does Texas Recognize Common Law Marriages From Other States In Regard To Divorce?

Not really. If there was a cause of action where another state, be it another judge or jury, had to enter the question where they common law married. For instance, if there was a lawsuit where someone is sued and the judge or jury had to decide if both parties could be liable because they're married and a trier of fact decided they are married, it would be recognized.

For common law marriage to be established for the first time, those three acts mentioned earlier, in Texas, at the same time, held themselves out to be husband and wife; or as things change, husband and husband, or wife and wife, but it has to be in Texas. Attorneys will also recognize somebody who has already made the determination that the marriage existed and they're still married.

In Texas, you also have a 2-year statute of limitations, and so your attorney will see if that applies or they try to get divorced after the 2 years and run, but whether that would really apply would be subject to a lot of litigation.

Divorce Process And Issues That Need To Be Handled In A 'Typical' Divorce

There is no such thing as a typical divorce, but there are generalities. If a person is, what they're called now, an unrepresented litigant, their divorce process can last up to almost a year, 270 days plus if it's the kind of the general or the typical divorce. Basically what happens is you meet with your divorce lawyer, you plan your process, and a divorce petition is filed. In Texas, they have electronic filing.

When lawyers file the divorce, at some point during the day, probably the next day, the district clerk's office or the county clerk's office who have that jurisdiction will open up that file, file mark it and send this to file mark copy back. At that point, the

lawyer will mail that divorce petition with a waiver of service for the citation to the other party and simply advise them that this is what they want, speak to an attorney if you want; if not, sign it or let them know where they want to proceed. The lawyers will wait a few days and serve them.

At that point the lawyers will start establishing what assets, what liabilities are, and they start framing out the divorce decree, but what the lawyers are really trying to work on is that 60 day process. You cannot get a divorce absent domestic violence in Texas unless it's 60 days. In the case if you have domestic violence, you can. For obvious reasons, you want to distance these people as soon as possible and getting some official orders, but absent that.

If you have to serve somebody for divorce, they have 20 days plus the following Monday, 10 am to respond. Lawyers are actually trying to work what is called 27 days possibly end of that 60 days so they can get the divorce petition, file it, get the final decree of divorce; they start drafting it. That'll have the assets, the liabilities, the children issues, the child support issues.

What Are Children's Issues In A Divorce Case?

Children's issues are who has the right to establish where the children stay, who has the visitation, what the schedule is, and that's based on how old the children are. The state of Texas has standard visitation schedules, but most lawyers don't subscribe to that. The office of Bobby Barina tailors them more to the parties based on how the children are, not necessarily by their age but how well they're able to understand what is going on.

A 16-year old child is going to drive back and forth to visitation, a 17-year old child is the same way. The court is going to treat them much differently than a 2-year old child or a child who's under the age of 1 who is possibly being breastfed. These are all totally different situations and they will have to be addressed accordingly.

Once the 60 days have passed, the lawyer will set in a court date for an agreed or default divorce. Default divorce is where they've been served, they refused to participate; it happens that what they're really saying is, "Hey, I know what's going to happen, I press my spouse to be fair," and we are fair. We telegraph everything to that other party. Telegraph means there is nothing hidden, they know exactly what we're doing, they've seen the final decree of divorce, they know when the lawyers are going to be in court and that's really the meat and potatoes of divorce.

In a divorce case where another lawyer comes in and becomes contested, then you really start to move away from the typical case. If they file discovery in a case, written discovery, they can blow it out or the first lawyer can blow it out to 180 days just by filing one piece of paper. That's difficult, that's when lawyers are arguing about things, so your attorney will try to resolve it. In the meantime, it is no longer than a general typical divorce.

Your attorney will work around the 60 days. At times when the lawyer talks to their client and everything goes perfectly, can it be over? A good lawyer will usually tell them 75 to 80 days to give some cushion room for some possible tinkering with the decrees.

Is There Any Way To Fast Track A Divorce?

Yes. But that's usually a give and take situation if the other party knows why. There are many reasons. A lot of it has to do with if a person's going to be eligible for more contributions from his employer for retirement contributions at a certain point, whether they become vested or not, there are some days that trip along.

In other cases, when you deal with military retirement, once they're married for 10 years while they service member, if serving his country for 10 years, then the retirement payments come directly from DFAS, our department of defense financial board. And so that's always a big date. But the best way to fast-track something is to really just stay on top of it. You file the divorce, you get the petition and the moment you get it, you mail it out. The moment you get the confirmation, the mail then received, you've established another letter of communication.

A lot of the younger people don't check their mail, and it has to be sent by email. It has to be locked in a PDF form so it's not altered, but the attorney can send it in the PDF with comments. At times, they'll ask their attorney for what something means, and the attorney cannot explain it to them if he doesn't represent them.

That's really the best way to fast-track something to stay on top of it in a non-accretive manner to be professional. Pay attention to the assets, how the lawyers are wishing them to be divided and then take them to the courthouse at the first opportunity. To get it under 60 days is not possible, but to fast-track it, the best way is to just stay on top of it and let the client know if that's what they want. They have to get this information back to the lawyers about what these assets are, who holds the note on the house, who holds the financing on the cars immediately.

The Most Common Reasons That People Cite For Divorce

There are many reasons that people cite for divorce. The most common reasons tend to be financial, they disagree on what to do, and they've grown apart. Texas has a no fault divorce, also called Insupportability. People look at that and say, "We just want to go our different ways", or, "Our careers have taken different directions. I am going to end up having a move or go back to school, we can't decide what to do about our children."

There are a lot of people who are too young, and there are also fault days where you're dealing with adultery, cruelty, things of that nature, but really the common reason is, "We simply don't wish to be married to each other anymore because we've grown apart. We're no longer compatible."

Is There A Divorce Client Seen More Often Than Others?

Currently, in Central Texas, Fort Hood is the largest military base in the free world, and has a very young population.

There are also a number of local schools and colleges where you see young people, around 21 to 25, both male or female, and they're just really starting to establish themselves financially, and that's when they realize, "We met, there were some things going on and we were very compatible with each other in the point we were in our lives. But now, we begin to explore where our careers are going to go, what our thoughts about when we'll have children," and they realize they've grown apart.

In such cases, it's usually seen when they're young and then there is a gap and then they're a little bit older, 35 to 40, where they've already gone through that cycle of establishing who they are and they're starting to return home or the nest is empty, the children have moved out of the home and then they come back to where they're needing divorce because they're no longer compatible and they just don't want to be married because there's nothing to keep them together anymore.

Do Men And Women View Divorce Differently?

They are very different. Really, they are different among women and different among men. When you look at a woman who is coming into a divorce situation and they're in the workforce or they're not in the workforce or if they have children, they view it very differently.

When the men come in, it's the same as the wife; they have children or they don't have the children, and they view the divorce very differently. But men tend to want to look at it like, "Okay, we're getting divorced now. There are going to be these major changes," and we kind of have to pull them back into thinking about this as a process that's ongoing.

Divorce really never ends if you have children; if you don't have children, then attorneys look at it just for dividing the property and women tend to look at it like they don't want certain aspects of their life to change. If they were stay-at-home, for example, they prefer to have the resources to continue that.

There is going to be somebody else who is going to have the children with them, so they're not going to have the children fulltime. And because they're going to have the children with them at least 35 to 41 percent of the time, during or after they enter the job force, they have to think about how that's going to go. Men still can reenter the job force much more easily than women do.

So, if women are outside the job market for a little bit, the skills they have in what they're doing tend to become dated, much like a cell phone. A cell phone changes over time as the technology changes, and that's how the job markets move as well. For some reason, men just seem to be able to enter more easily because it seems to be more acceptable, and women find it difficult to go back in the same position they were before.

How Is A Successful Outcome In A Divorce Case Defined?

It's hard to say that there is a winner and a loser, but there are cases where the attorney is required to meet the goals as given to them by their clients, and that's a success where they work together, they come up with the list of goals and objectives, and they meet them. Once the attorney gets a chance to talk to the clients, they look at what realistic goals are.

Many times, you'll have a client who says, "I want the house," but they don't make enough to pay for the house. What if they take the house, which is worth a good deal of money, and the other party takes cash and other things that aren't subject to capital gains taxes? What if the client can't pay for the house and suddenly they have to sell it, so they sell it for a good chunk of change and then they're hit with the capital gains and suddenly they're broke? The successful outcome starts with goals and objectives. The client has to explore them together with their attorney and they discuss how to meet those goals.

In a child custody situation, a successful outcome is reached where you can look down the road and say, “This child is going to grow up in a loving environment and is going to have the best possibility to succeed and be a contributing member of our society and influence others around them in a very positive way.”

Success is looking at parental differences. Some of them have greater strengths and an attorney needs that ability to look at it to make sure you know which ones they are. Success is deciding which parent should have the child, whether it’s the client or not, and that can take a great deal of persuasion to get both parties to see your point of view.

There are ways to make their message known even to their representative party by the things attorneys say in court, the things they say in their negotiations, and the things they say in their mediation process as they roll together before they break up in separate limbs. That’s how success is defined—in meeting those goals.

Common Questions Asked By People Planning To File For Divorce

There are a number of questions that people planning to file for divorce ask their attorneys. Some of these questions are as following:

Would You Need A Valid Reason To File For Divorce In Texas?

For a long time, in the state of Texas couples had to have a valid reason but right now, it's simply insupportability, or the clients saying we do not wish to be married. As long as somebody says that during the final prove up, that is enough.

The reason is that the state of Texas decided 'No, we're going to stop putting people through this.' They don't wish to be married. Why have them give a reason to somebody; in other words, to say they just weren't good to me, this is all their fault in open court where their children would know and would make them bitter and you have to get along with them, make them bitter for years.

Are There Any Benefits Of Filing For Divorce Before Your Spouse?

There really is, and it becomes lesser everyday by the emergence of what we call 'Standing Orders.' Standing Orders are what judges and courts like to use to say, "When you file for divorce, these are the rules you have to live by."

Once your spouse gets served with the divorce papers, it's part of the paperwork and they're ordered to play by the same rules, not dissipate the assets, not to incur more bills unless it's for business or living expenses, not to remove the children from the location, and not to disenfranchise or move or lock your spouse out of the family home and tell the court.

Despite all this, there still is the reason to go first. You've made a decision, you're prepared for it emotionally, financially, as best you can but it means that you file first, you have the first ability to ask for what we call ex parte orders from the court.

The ex-party orders will last 10 days until you get to court, but it means you go first in every instance unless there is a temporary hearing that they've asked for, but on the divorce process, you go first. You dictate the flow of when things get done and that, if you're in the receiving end of that, that's some of the unknown, that's some of the uncertainty. You call your lawyer, "Hey, when are we going to go to court?", "Well, let me talk to this other person and get things set." There is still communication, but the petitioner is really in the seat of doing most of the scheduling, and that's an important part.

Can You File For Custody First And Does It Allow You Any Control Or Advantage In Custody?

Yes. If you do file first, and the temporary orders that are in effect or the standing orders state that you don't change where the children are living. Well, what if you file and you have access to that home, you kept the children with you? And that's really what it's about.

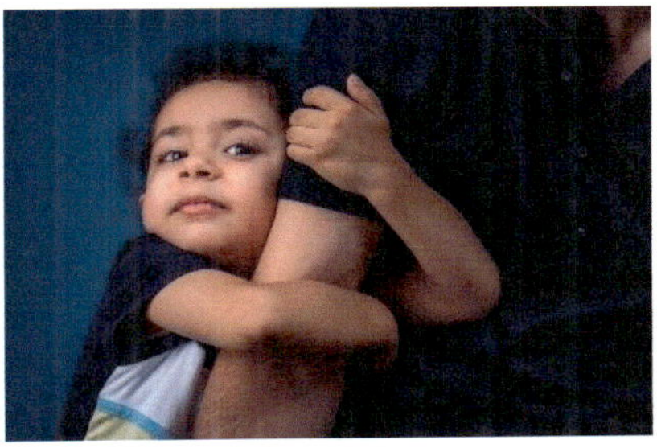

Let's say that you filed during the summer and it's agreed that children would stay with you for the summer, or they're down here at a different location and you file while the children are with you. And the thought process on that is that it prevents the children from having to deal with important issues because you won't drag it out in front of them, you won't browbeat them, but also they're there with you and the judges like to maintain a sense of stability. So, there is a reason to file for the divorce first with the custody provisions and do it first.

Is There Any Required Period Of Separation Before Filing For Divorce In Texas?

None. Oddly enough, with people with less resources or young people, they're actually still in the same home during what we call the 60-day cooling off period. But they don't have to be separated before they file the divorce.

They simply say, "The date of the separation is the date of the filing the divorce where we're separated not necessarily physically but we've separated our intent, our persons from the marital union and we're separated in that sense that we no longer have the common goal to be married and to present ourselves to the world as husband and wife." So, no, there is no period required for them to be separated.

Is It Recommend To File For An Uncontested Divorce If There Really Is Nothing To Divide Up?

Not really. In Texas, we just have divorce. They don't have the ability to designate in the title uncontested; what they do have are three phases of discovery. And these three phases are for divorce or for the large commercial transactions, for community trust suits, and for lawsuits against corporations.

When you look at it, the first phase is for property under $50,000. If you're talking about how much they have in assets and if you file it there, you have different rules; if you file it in phase 2 or discovery level 2, which is the most common for family law, then you're saying there's children or there are assets over $50,000. And it becomes uncontested if a process develops where there is no difference or disagreement between what an attorney will propose from their client to the respondent.

That's how the attorney will file if something that develops as a process as they go through the divorce. And they put out their client's goals and what they want from the divorce in writing and agreed final order of divorce. If the other party agrees with that, then it is uncontested.

Can A Divorce Be Filed Without Having To Let Your Spouse Know?

Absolutely. In Texas, there are many different areas to file. If you're living in the county for the required period of time, you can file a divorce. Usually, where a lawyer or the party sends a waiver of service of citation, service is where they place the citation, notice of the lawsuit in the other spouse's hand, that's when the spouse is notified.

They can mail that to them, just say, "Hi, I am divorcing you," where you waive any further notice; or they can be served by a process server or somebody from local law enforcement who's last moved to the state of Texas. A Texas-certified peace officer to serve them with the divorce but there are many cases where somebody files a divorce, they leave it pending for a good period of time and then they'll notify the spouse. Once the spouse is notified, they have an amount of time to respond to the lawsuit, so you just can't notify them and go into the court the next day. But you can file it and not tell anybody.

There are websites to tell you who has done what and who has filed what in most instances. Domestic abuse protective orders would be an instance where it's shielded but yes, you can definitely do the divorce process.

Can Someone File For A U.S. Divorce If They Were Married In Another Country?

Absolutely, that is done all the time. It's really a very fluid trend in a society where people travel so often. If you get divorced elsewhere and you have a valid marriage license from that other state or other jurisdiction, then if you're in Texas for 6 months, a resident of Bell County for instance, or any other county where you live for 90 days to proceed to file the divorce, you can get divorced here.

The only problem that ever comes into trying to divide assets that may exist in a foreign country, and you just have to take your time with that. Sometimes discovery in another country is limited by that other country's domestic law, and so you just have to comply with that.

The office of Bobby Barina has many different kind of attorneys throughout the Boroughs; some are called barristers, solicitors, and so they just ask for a derogatory to discover what the assets are over there and it just takes a little bit more time and service is also a little bit unusual. Sometimes, lawyers have to use the Hague convention to serve a foreign national if only one of the parties is here. The office of Bobby Barina can definitely do that.

Does It Just Have To Be That 6 Months?

Yes, 6 months in the state and 90 days in the county.

Can A Spouse Refuse To Sign Divorce Papers?

Yes, absolutely. No one is going to force them to do it because that's their right to do it alone. When the lawyers at Bobby Barina's office have a spouse who does not sign it, the lawyers do not apply any pressure. If that spouse refuses to sign, that's their right and they can hire an attorney.

They can represent themselves but at that point, attorneys have the process server or a member of local law enforcement who will professionally give them the paperwork, fill out an affidavit so the judge and the district clerk's office and the world would know that they know of this divorce process. Attorneys wait the requisite amount of time and they set it for a hearing on that petition for a divorce and they simply proceed with or without them.

Once the judge has ruled, their signature is not really required. The lawyers put a paragraph in there. If they do sign it, they know what it says, if they don't sign it, you don't have that paragraph.

What Steps Can An Attorney Take To Assist Someone's Spouse In Accusing Them Of Abuse Either For Financial Gain Or For Custody?

That's the informal discovery process. The law office has formal discovery where they ask depositions, questions or participating depositions and written questions but in that process, they talk to family and friends, and get a list of witnesses. After that, they give out forms for these witnesses to get the rough overview of what they would say. Have they seen signs of abuse, have they seen the client with the child or children, etc., and what they would say, and then the lawyers go through it to zero in on that person.

Sometimes, the attorneys send an investigator out to talk to people and they look for as many different witnesses as possible who will tell the truth, that this didn't happen, that this person is lying, and then they take a closer look at the financial stability of the parties to see if that might be a motivating factor. They'll ask them questions under oath, but really it's just sitting down, talking to the client, finding out what happened, what the possible motivation is, and then proceeding further to run down the evidence necessary. That's really what it is: Finding the evidence, bringing it to the courtroom in a timely fashion, letting the judge hear it in a coherent way.

The more prepared you are, the less likely you're going to have a contested hearing. That's just the nature of the base, nobody wants to go in there when the outcome is so predetermined. You're prepared, you want to be more prepared than the other party, you want to have your witnesses there and the other party will simply say in a lot of cases, "This isn't worth it, let's move on to Plan B to see if we can go a different route."

What Is Better, Mediation Or The Court Process When Handling A Divorce?

Mediation always has a great deal of attractiveness to the law, but it depends on a couple of things. First of all, mediation is useless if the other party is unreasonable. If the other party has not been able to distance themselves from the emotional context of it, and if the other party is represented by an attorney who does not have the ability to keep them informed as to what their options are, then it becomes useless.

When Is Mediation A Good Option? How Do Mediators Help?

If the two parties are ready to end the marriage, are ready to talk about what's best for the children, then mediation is absolutely the best process. Getting ready for mediation is the same as getting ready for court. You have to have all the information; when the mediator's going back and forth, he has to be able to discuss coherently, rationally, and quickly.

We gather information about the property, the child's situation, everything off the top of his head, and prepare all that evidence. Here are the witnesses who would say this, this, and this. But once that's established, the parties will start to resolve their marriage, through the use of the mediator, based on someone's input and directions that being the mediator who's gotten the chance to know them.

Once the mediator gets to say, "Hello, who are you? Where do you come from? Where did you grow up? Where did you go to high school?" And in a very professional way, "How's that panned out for you? Do you want to get back to that ground? How are you going to get that job? What are the children going to do? What's the school process? Do children have any special needs?" He's now asked more than the judge will ever get to know. He is now vested in their success; the judge never is.

The judge will simply enter a ruling that children go over there, the assets go here, it's done. The mediator will help them craft the decision that they participated in. If they have the opportunity to participate in the outcome and they're vested in it, it is the outcome that will stay on the test of time, that it will be a case where they will go back to court only for the smallest of issues. They won't go to rehash things, they won't go to say, "You know what? I didn't really want to do that because they participated." They didn't have anything forced down their throats.

But all these things have to exist first before mediation can be successful and with the mediator, like anything else, there are different levels of talents, there are different personalities involved. For instance, considering some personalities, if one party is strong-willed, then you may want to get a mediator who has the ability to talk to strong-willed people, to talk about child issues more than property issues, to talk about autism, special education, and talk about a favorable interest rate or favorable return on investment. So, each mediator will have a strong point.

Lawyers have to direct the parties to the right mediator to address those parties' needs, and sometimes the lawyer themselves will mediate. If one of them is better for child custody, the lawyer will do that portion, and then they'll go to a mediator who is really skilled in the ability of property division, who understands how the stock market is in a great state of flux, how you really can't buy into that necessarily full force, that you might have to take cash, you might have to take a discount, present values. Sometimes lawyers even use two mediators.

Importance Of Hiring An Attorney In A Divorce Case

There are many reasons people should hire an attorney instead of trying to do it themselves.

I had a friend who was a teacher and a brilliant young lady. She did her own divorce, did everything, and over the years, she was always having to come back to court to tinker with it to fix something and so every time she had to go back to court, it opened up all the old wounds and for months afterwards, they couldn't get along.

Also, while you know you'll have to go back to court possibly for child support or for some changes in the portion dealing with the children, you should never have to really go back concerning the two of you,

and that's the reason you want to hire an attorney. If your spouse has an attorney, you don't want to deal with that other lawyer. And if you don't think the spouse has been reasonable, you definitely need a lawyer.

Why Should A Couple Hire Separate Divorce Attorneys Instead Of Hiring One Attorney?

You're hiring somebody to look out for you and you alone, not to look out for the two of you. When an attorney is hired, they owe their ability, their loyalty, to one person. And when they go through the interview process, they get to know the person, it's specifically tailored to the reaction of that one person. For instance, do you have any concerns? What do you want out of these proceedings? The answer is going to be different for both parties.

When someone has a meeting with a lawyer, they have to discover your skills, where you are going to live, what support network you have; those type of questions and answers. Clearly, the answers aren't going to be the same for both, and so you need somebody to advocate your point of view to push your goals and your outcome.

That's why you want your own lawyer; to ask things like whether you were the victim of domestic abuse, or are you somebody who is going to have to leave the job market to reenter the job market. Well, your husband may not want to pay for that or your wife may not want to pay for that, but here's why you're entitled to it.

You are buying somebody's faith and their loyalty to you to do the best they can for you, and you really can't go without that. When you live in a world where so many people fall below the poverty line after divorce, this is like buying a house, truly a long term-decision that has many ramifications. Divorce is one of the most serious aspects that we deal with in our lives, and when that happens to more than 50 percent of the population who gets the divorce, you want somebody who is only looking out for you.

Do People Underestimate The Divorce Process, Both Emotionally And Financially?

Yes, they do. When people consult an attorney, it takes time to really establish a relationship. The whole process takes time before both the client and lawyer decide they are going to enter into an attorney/client relationship. They're still going through the process of getting to know each other, the client discovering how he or she can best manage what the client needs. At some point, the attorney will just break it down to them.

What they're looking at is marriage as X's and O's, it's all about love, divorce is all about one's zeros; it's business. People often forget what the lawyer is going to do for them, they look at it and they want to trust their spouse to be fair. In the area of Central Texas, where Bobby Barina practices, there are so many different types of cases; they have the military, they have medical complexes, and then a short distance away they have the tech industries.

There are so many different benefits that they're supposed to divide. The average person doesn't know about that if they're not getting the benefits, and they don't know

they are supposed to get a division of it and so they let that go because it was a simple divorce, and they didn't want to pay somebody to ask these questions, they didn't want to pay somebody to get in there and look this information up.

Their spouse may say, "Hey, I've been working here a year. Here is how much I have invested." Well, what he didn't tell you is what happens if he goes the next year and he gets more of a contribution. What is to be done then? There is no such thing as a simple divorce until you have all the information and that client can knowingly say these are the options, hear us out, perhaps I will take it.

There are also divorce cases where marriages last less than a year, so no community property has been bought. It's a pretty quick process to run down a credit report to look up if the community card's open revolving credit accounts and bank accounts and make a determination. But generally, there is not an easy divorce. In a divorce you make decisions only after knowing what all of your options are.

What Misconceptions Do People Have About Working With An Attorney Through A Divorce?

There are many misconceptions, but the common one is that the attorney is going to be too expensive, they're simply there to take their money, they don't care, they're looking to make the process dragged out for more money or possibly go too quickly and not really take the time to get to know somebody.

These are the kinds of misconceptions that the office of Bobby Barina has to deal with when clients are brought in to their initial consultation.

A lot of people come in and simply think a divorce is nothing but paperwork, and that's all. That's one of the major misconceptions when people try to do it themselves. Attorneys not here just for paperwork, they're here to explore options, to find out who their clients are, to tailor a process that's specific to them and their needs and also their family's needs.

Attorney Bobby Barina's Experience In Divorce Law

Bobby Dale Barina has been a lawyer since 1991 and has been practicing family law since 1996. What really led him to do family laws is it was the part of the law that he saw people do, and it led him to help people.

Before that, he was doing criminal law only, and now he does criminal and family, but family law is his primary focus. The types of lawsuits he practices are divorce, establishment of paternity child custody, child support, terminations, and more. He is board certified in family law by the Texas Board of Legal Specialization and has been board certified since 2002.

What Experience Does Attorney Bobby Barina Have In Divorce Law?

Bobby Barina is a Texas super lawyer; he has a 'cape' in everything. If he could really dress up handling a super lawyer SL, he would. In his office he has the eagle wall, which is spread in the entire span of the office displaying every award he has been given. Every one of those was earned by having a relationship with a client that he's learned something and made their life a little bit better.

Bobby Barina says, 'I can point at every one of them and say, "Here is why we got it placed is because somebody came in, trust me enough to give me these resources, this money to look after that." And I think that is so important. And I really like what I do, I really do.'

What Sets The Law Firm of Bobby Barina Apart From Other Family Law Attorneys?

There are a lot of lawyers who do divorces. Just because someone's qualified to do something doesn't make them an expert. You can go to a doctor, a general practitioner; that doesn't make them an expert to look at cancer situations, to do surgeries, and it's the same thing in law. Just because someone's qualified by having a bar license or a bar card, an attorney's license on the wall, doesn't mean they're an expert in divorce.

Attorney Bobby Barina is divorced, he's gone through child custody, gone through property division. He understands how this process works and he can really bring a personal touch and a lot of experience. His law firm is dealing with these issues on a daily basis and that's what he shares with the clients when they're talking to him.

Sometimes, he'll cut them off a little bit and say, "Hi, we're getting to feel a little bit." This isn't the emotional context right now. But to help steer them back to what goals and objectives he can help them with, it's that initial communication, it's that sitting with them. You have a lot of lawyers that have the big debt that separates them.

Bobby's firm will start off by writing stuff down. And then they'll move over there with them and talk to them, because this really is a relationship. And that's what the law firm is giving them. It's a relationship with somebody who, for a short period of their life, is going to guide them through this valley of darkness, which is really the volume and certainty.

Bobby Barina's firm is going to guide them through it from the beginning of the process to the very end, and at the very end, they're going to understand what they went through, what happened to them, what they've accomplished and the rules that they've established on how they're going to live their life for the foreseeable future. These things really set the firm apart from any others because of their experience.

When someone goes to another lawyer's office, they're going to have different experiences and different ways of meeting that out. Most people are going to get somebody who gives them a few forms, and that's a best state to pond them off but to move them to a different phase to where they're dealing only with the assistant who is doing all the paperwork, that's not the relationship.

That's what Bobby Barina will offer in that relationship. And the clients have to believe that Bobby is with them every step of the way, or they're going to doubt the advice that he gives them.

With the given advice, it's not just based on child winning or the position of finances in the world, it's also that the lawyer has seen this judge before. He knows what that judge wants, because while attorneys are not able to speak to the judge privately about an ongoing case, they can surely sit in that courtroom on a daily basis and watch that judge make decisions and ask questions in cases very similar to the ones Bobby's firm has represented.

Bobby is going to be able to tell them when they're pushing a bad position, or when that's just something they're not going to get out of these goals, and he'll be able to tell them why. They are going to have to adjust their presentation of the evidence in a little bit different manner to meet this judge's goals.

Bobby's office has had cases where they've had to spend money and tell the client, "We're going to have to spend money to get these things put in a different form." In other words, pie-charts and visual aids, because the connection we need to have with this judge is more in writing than it is orally.

The judge will remember it, respect it, maintain it more if he sees it in this modality and receives it instead of orally. That's what Bobby's firm is giving them, and if they don't trust the attorney, then they don't have a longstanding relationship, and there is not much the attorney can do for them. The attorney really can't get them to buy into it about what's best for their future as a suggestion from them.

DISCLAIMER

This publication is intended to be informational only. The information in this book is not intended as legal advice. No legal advice is being given, and no attorney-client relationship is intended to be created by reading this material. If you are facing legal issues, whether criminal or civil, seek professional legal counsel to get your questions answered.

Bobby Dale Barina,

455 E. Central Texas Expy

Suite 104

Harker Heights, TX 76548

(254) 870-9947

www.yourkilleendivorceattorney.com

Made in the USA
Monee, IL
05 November 2026

67386568R00038